Alone in the Burning

poems

Wendy McVicker

Sheila-Na-Gig Editions

ACKNOWLEDGMENTS

My deep gratitude to Hayley Mitchell Haugen, who published the first of these poems ("When I was alone, clouds") in slightly different form in *Sheila-Na-Gig online* when I wasn't sure they were more than splinters; to Claire Bateman, who saw the first batch of these splinters, and encouraged me to keep writing them; to Pauletta Hansel and her 2022 manuscript class, for invaluable help in honing and persistence; to my poetry community, for listening and feedback and encouragement, whether in the woods or by the sea or on our porches and computer screens. None of us is here alone.

And, always, thanks to my beloved family, for steadfast patience and good humor while sharing their lives with a poet.

for HSB, who told me the truth

CONTENTS

Lost

Here we have a sister and her brothers, each one alone in the burning house. All doors locked. There are peonies outside the windows, covered in sticky ants, but the only scent is of smoke and gas. Beyond the creaking walls circles a creature who has swallowed time. They can hear ticking as it stalks. The children flew to enter this world, but here they found only danger. Where are the grownups? Lost, too. How to tell this story from the heart of the fire? How far must we fly to escape the embers?

> The alphabet a rope
>   slipping through my hands
>   each word a knot, burning

When I was alone

clouds breathed

leaves in the trees
breathed
through my dreams

small grasses
pebbles
the mica-flecked stream

they all breathed
with me

When I was alone

I ciphered the alphabet

on sills below windows
that opened to jungle

one sentence
one tree was all

it took to fly

When I was alone

light slanted
through a mansion
hidden in the woods

Glass fine as sand
sifted across the floor

and shadows
hummed ghosts
on the stairs

Out on the curved drive
a snake coiled
and uncoiled

a message
I could not read

When I was alone

I knew how to hold
still, hold stillness
close to my heart

I knew how to wait:
one way to be safe

Running is another:
not my way

In the story the doe
broke and ran
across the clearing

That's when the gun
found her

That's how I learned
to be still

That's how I learned
to wait

When I was alone

I slipped into cracks
between bricks

hid behind doors
that slammed

and in the deep
closet   air thick

with Saturday night
perfume

hidden
I read

the first stories
the first maps

Unearthed (1)

A dim, yellow-green light like a kind of veil, made of cold dark rain and the dread that lived in that house, fills the room. It gathers in dusty vases and behind the picture on the wall, where a twisty road leads into the hills, and dizzying ground rises to a wild sky.

The child, age four, with chopped cropped hair and a thumb never far from her mouth, wanders the vast green sea of the rug, with its tendrils that may be plants, or eyeless creatures with wavery tentacles. Rain streaks down the glass, the air in the room tightens.

When I was alone

stars fell on my face
in the back
of the old DeSoto

From the front seat
their voices singing
mournful and slow

Show me the way
to go home

By morning
the song was over

and the stars
had blown away

When I was alone

sparkles
on her party
dress: black sequins

all around her skirt
spun like records

They went out dancing

Sometimes
he carried her home

When I was alone

two more came along
in the February dawn

They shared
a common language

only I could interpret
for the grownups

No one speaks it
anymore

When I was alone

I was not alone,
we were three

We rocked
forward and back
forward and back

on the scratchy
couch
We called it
bouncing

Two, or maybe
all three, sucked
our thumbs

Mornings were brittle,
easily shattered

We bounced
and sucked

When I was alone

so many ways breath
caught in the throat

unfiltered cigarettes
that raw burn

seeping of gas
under the sill

Without breath
there can be no words

Without words
no —

Unearthed (2)

The air in the room tightens, gas seeps serpentine along the rug, the clouded linoleum, hisses as it presses at locked doors, turns dark air to lead in the child's chest.

Where is everyone?

When I was alone

no cellar   no attic
no stairs
going up or down

That house was a flat
box   and still

I found places
to hide

When I was alone

a fortress
could be made of pillows
or blocks or sometimes
piles of books

Pillows muffled sounds
it was better not
to hear

Blocks blocked
the view

Books formed causeways
through the swamp

away
from the rising tide

When I was alone

the grownups were lost
in a far-off world

the piano
brought them closer:

ladders of sound
I climbed

to reach them

When I was alone

a cave
under the piano
filled with sound

Her hands were busy
on the keys

They couldn't reach
me there

Unearthed (3)

Where is everyone?

Her mother, locked again in the bedroom, her tiny brothers quiet in their cribs. The walls of the house bulge and constrict around her. Her chest, too, tightens, her throat burns.

When I was alone

lightning struck the chimney
of the neighbors' house

I heard the grownups
talking in ragged
voices

about the way lightning
would strike

sudden
out of the blue

It sounded familiar
I felt that forked fire

all the way
through my body

throat
to molten core

When I was alone

I escaped into dusk

let that honeysuckle air
cool my skin

I twirled
on the green
green grass until

I was lassoed
and yanked back in

to the blazing
house

When I was alone

tiger lilies lined up
along the wall

orange patches nodding
in the gloom

A crocodile circled the dark
lagoon

In that story the children
were lost

(and never found)

When I was alone

a bird fell
into the uncut grass

Our father, who
could not hold
what he most wanted

held the bird
gentled its feathers

felt it pulse
between his palms

After some days
in a corner
of the kitchen

it found the sky

When I was alone

it was my job to save
the lost boys

I could not

Unearthed (4)

Her chest tightens, her throat burns. A hard grip coils around her ribs, squeezes. When her father arrives at last, he pounds on the locked door, he shouts, "She can't breathe, she can't breathe." That was almost the end for the child and her brothers. Maybe for the mother, too. They all lived on, somehow. The mother slowly starved herself to death, sunk in silence.

When I was alone

things broke
windows
bottles

toys
sometimes
furniture

stories broke
over my head
and carried me
to a farther shore

later, bones,
later, hearts

You can walk around
for a long time
with a broken heart

and no one will notice
least of all
you

When I was alone

I found a box
of old books

in the cobwebby
garage

the walls were rough
powdery as chalk

tissue pages
watercolor pictures

each one a map
to another world

I folded and re-folded
their soft paper

tales of intrepid
girls crossing

the sea   facing
into the wind

That was the day
my life began

and when it was time
I was gone

Found

This is a story about a girl who learned to live in books. It started when her father read to her: he was an alchemist who transformed black marks on the page into living worlds he and she could enter and explore, worlds where they could laugh together. The sad stories came later, when she had learned the magic of alchemy herself. In one, chicks went wandering far from the barn and came back late, found the door locked. They all died, huddled against that unyielding wood. Wendy and her brothers flew in from Neverland, to find the casement windows closed and themselves replaced in the nursery. Does this story have a moral? That is what she is still trying to find out.

> Language held the key
> Long strings of letters flying
> off the page took her with them

When I was alone

the sky was as big
as memory

This has been
a long journey

Clouds still form
at the horizon

Sometimes, rain

Wendy McVicker, 2020-2022 poet laureate of Athens, Ohio, is a longtime Ohio Arts Council teaching artist. Her previous books include *the dancer's notes* (Finishing Line Press, 2015), the self-published collaboration with visual artist John McVicker *Sliced Dark* (2019), *Zero, a Door* (The Orchard Street Press, 2021), and *Stronger When We Touch*, a collaboration with poet Cathy Cultice Lentes (The Orchard Street Press, 2023). She loves collaborating with artists in many media and performs with instrumentalist Emily Prince under the name "another language altogether" whenever she gets the chance. Her children having grown and flown, she lives surrounded by the green hills of southeastern Ohio with her husband and a Hemingway cat named Dora.

Sheila-Na-Gig Editions

www.ingramcontent.com/pod-product-compliance
Lightning Source LLC
Chambersburg PA
CBHW061328120626
46546CB00007B/2725